Library of Congress Catalog – in Publication Data:

An application to register this book for cataloging has been submitted to the Library of Congress.

ISBN-13: 978-0692963784 (Graced 2 Finish Publishing, LLC)

ISBN-10: 0692963782

This book was printed in the United States of America.

Cover design and book layout by: A. Payne's Designs
amber@apaynedesigns.com

Editing by: UpgradeU Writing and Editing Services
info@upgradeuediting.com

Acknowledgements

I dedicate this book to my grandparents, Mr. Albert Ray Walters and Mrs. Letha Mae Berry Walters who would have been so proud to see that all of my years of reading and writing finally caused me to become a published author. To my parents, Drs. Gerald and Vivian Morgan, my husband, children, and all of my extended family and friends who always asked me, "When are you going to write that book!", I say THANK YOU! Your prayers and support meant so much to me during this process. To every aspiring writer, never stop writing! Someone is waiting to hear your voice. Pen it!

Birthing of This Devotional Journal
Origin of the Seek, Apply, Share (S.A.S.) Principle

One day, I was studying the Word and thinking about how important it is for us to share with others what we learn. The words seek, apply, and share came to mind. This is where the S.A.S. Principle came from. This principle will help you grow to maturity and inspire others to do the same in their walk with the Lord. Let's look at the definition of each word.

Seek

- To go in search or quest of
- To try to find or discover by searching or questioning
- To try to obtain
- To try or attempt
- To go to
- To ask for; request
- To search or explore

Apply

- To make use of as relevant, suitable or pertinent
- To put to use, especially for a particular purpose
- To bring into action; use; employ
- To use a label or other designation
- To use for or assign to a specific purpose
- To put into effect
- To devote or employ diligently or with close attention
- To place in contact with; lay or spread on
- To bring into physical contact with or close proximity
- To credit to, as an account

Share

- The full or proper portion or part allotted or belonging to or contributed cr owed by an individual group
- One of the equal fractional parts into which capital stock of a joint stock company or corporation is divided
- To divide and distribute in shares; apportion
- To use; participate in; enjoy, receive

Principles are an accepted rule or professed rule of action or conduct. It is also defined as a fundamental, primary or general law or truth from which others are derived.

How To Use This Devotional Journal

When we look at the words seek, apply, and share from a biblical standpoint, we will find that the S.A.S. Principle lines up with what we are already commanded to do. The other important component to the S.A.S. Principle is that this works only for those who are committed to making changes in their own personal lives. There can be no transformation without the renewing of the mind, and the S.A.S. Principle is a tool to be used to get you there and encourage others to do the same. It is also a great tool for evangelism and discipleship and encourages you to share your faith daily in a practical way.

So, if you are ready to take the challenge of being all God created you to be, let the S.A.S. Principle be your guide. Determine a set time that you will work through this devotional journal. Sit in a quiet place with no distractions. Pray before you begin and ask the Holy Spirit to open up revelation to you. Soak in His Presence as He ministers to you. Sip on a cup of tea. Diffuse some essential oils. Ready? Set? Go! It's a new day! Daybreak is here! Think like a champion!

Think like a champion!

Over the next 30 days, take the journey through Romans 12:2 as we use the S.A.S. Principle to unlock life keys to help you tear down wrong mindsets and put on the mind of Christ. May you be endowed with the Spirit of the Lord, the spirit of wisdom and understanding, the spirit of counsel and might, and the fear of the Lord!

Let's go!

And be not conformed to this world: but be ye transformed by the renewing of your mind, that ye may prove what is that good, and acceptable, and perfect, will of God (Romans 12:2 KJV).

Don't copy the behavior and customs of this world, but let God transform you into a new person by changing the way you think. Then you will learn to know God's will for you, which is good and pleasing and perfect (Romans 12:2 NLT).

Table of Contents

Any time you are called to something, there is a corresponding action that must take place. When we are told not to do something, it is because it imposes danger upon our lives. There is a world standard in which we are born into. But, when we accept Jesus Christ as our Lord and Savior, there is a new birth that takes place. And this new birth brings us into a new way of living. The time in between these two events have fashioned us into the ways of the world. Our way of thinking, according to our intellect, is antithetical to the Mind of Christ, and it is this mold that we must break out of. We cannot operate from the old mindset in the new way of life. When I think of something being conformed, I imagine a mold and plaster. You are the mold and the world is the plaster. Whatever the plaster fills solidifies itself into the mold. It's just like being on the potter's wheel. Whatever molds you makes you a vessel for its use. If you are on the world's potter's wheel, you will be fashioned n the same pattern as a vessel to be used by the world's system. You will look like the world. You will speak like the world. You will hear like the world. You will walk like the world. However, once you are on the Lord's potter's wheel, He begins to reshape you into His vessel to be used as an ambassador for the Kingdom of God. And we can only be effective as His ambassadors by allowing a mindset shift to take place. We must respond to the call to action by going through the process of renewing our mind daily.

How will you respond?

S.A.S. Principle

*Romans 12:2 ~ **And be not conformed to this world:** but be ye transformed by the renewing of your mind, that ye may prove what is that good, and acceptable, and perfect, will of God.*

Write the Scripture:
Word Study: *"And be not conformed to this world"*

Seek

1. What is God speaking to you regarding this Scripture?

2. What questions or revelation do you seek to know?

3. What is the principle to be learned?

4. Write out a short affirmation to help you remember the principle that you have learned.

Apply

1. How does this passage apply to my life? (past or present)

Share

1. How can I share the principle with others in a practical way?

Journal additional thoughts here:

_____

_____

_____

_____

_____

Day Two Journey: Be Not

"And be not conformed to this world"

You will never be fashioned into His frame until you submit (come into complete obedience) to the mind renewal process. The words "be not" are command words. They are meant as words of instruction for the hearer to follow what comes after it. Like a parent instructs a child, it is important for us to take heed to these two words BE NOT. It should cause our ears and our spirit to come to attention so that we can hear the forthcoming instruction.

S.A.S. Principle

Romans 12:2 ~ And be not conformed to this world: but be ye transformed by the renewing of your mind, that ye may prove what is that good, and acceptable, and perfect, will of God.

Write the Scripture:

Word Study: "And be not conformed to this world"

Seek

1. What is God speaking to you regarding this Scripture?

2. What questions or revelation do you seek to know?

3. What is the principle to be learned?

4. Write out a short affirmation to help you remember the principle that you have learned.

Apply

1. How does this passage apply to my life? (past or present)

Share

1. How can I share the principle with others in a practical way?

Journal additional thoughts here:

_____

_____

_____

_____

_____

Day Three Journey: Morph Up!

"And be not conformed to this world"

To fashion your old mind to the renewed mind, one must Morph Up! What is morph up? Morph up is the metamorphosis that the old mind must go through to become the renewed mind. There must be a change from one state to another by natural or supernatural means. We must allow the Holy Spirit to do a reconstruction in our thoughts and behaviors. We must tear down our old thought patterns and behaviors so that we won't stay conformed to the old way of thinking. The old will always be beneath the new. So, I challenge you today to morph up and break out of the box of subpar living.

S.A.S. Principle

*Romans 12:2 ~ **And be not conformed to this world: but be ye transformed by the renewing of your mind, that ye may prove what is that good, and acceptable, and perfect, will of God.***

Write the Scripture:

Word Study: "And be not conformed to this world"

Seek

1. What is God speaking to you regarding this Scripture?

2. What questions or revelation do you seek to know?

3. What is the principle to be learned?

4. Write out a short affirmation to help you remember the principle that you have learned.

Apply

1. How does this passage apply to my life? (past or present)

Share

1. How can I share the principle with others in a practical way?

Journal additional thoughts here:

_____

_____

_____

_____

_____

Day Four Journey: Things To Avoid
"And be not conformed to this world"

Worldly contamination comes by not renewing our mind to the new life in Christ. A mind that is conformed to the world system makes us unsuitable and unusable in the Kingdom of God because we will not understand the principles of the Kingdom. Contamination breeds impurity. And impurity is not an attribute in the Kingdom. Matthew 5:8 says, "Blessed are the pure in heart, for they will see God." Out of the abundance of the heart, the mouth speaks. A contaminated heart cannot produce righteous thoughts. Unrighteous thoughts cannot produce righteous living.

S.A.S. Principle

Romans 12:2 ~ And be not conformed to this world: but be ye transformed by the renewing of your mind, that ye may prove what is that good, and acceptable, and perfect, will of God.

Write the Scripture:

Word Study: "And be not conformed to this world"

Seek

1. What is God speaking to you regarding this Scripture?

2. What questions or revelation do you seek to know?

3. What is the principle to be learned?

4. Write out a short affirmation to help you remember the principle that you have learned.

Apply

1. How does this passage apply to my life? (past or present)

Share

1. How can I share the principle with others in a practical way?

Journal additional thoughts here:

_____

_____

_____

_____

_____

Day Five Journey: This World vs. Your World

"And be not conformed to this world"

What exactly is this world? Why are we instructed to not be conformed to this world?

Before coming to Christ, there is a standard of this world that we are born into. And this world's standard is the opposite to the standard of the Lord. We saw in an earlier devotion that the words "be not" indicated a precursor to an instruction. This instruction alerts us to the danger of conforming to the world's system. First John 2:15-17 gives a warning of these worldly systems. There is a three-fold cord of wickedness: The lust of the flesh (2:16a), the lust of the eyes (2:16b), the pride of life (2:16c).

If we wrap our minds around these worldly systems and become entangled with this three-fold cord of wickedness, we will fade away with them. Having a worldly mindset is worthless to the kingdom of light. It has no ability to produce the glory of God as it is only consumed with pleasing self. And when we are consumed with loving and pleasing self, there is no room for the love of The Father. But by making a commitment to daily mind renewal, we have the ability to shed off layers of wrong thinking by allowing the love of the Father to shine the light on the dark areas and bring transformation. Don't forfeit eternity by holding on to that which has no eternal gain.

S.A.S. Principle

Romans 12:2 ~ And be not conformed to this world: but be ye transformed by the renewing of your mind, that ye may prove what is that good, and acceptable, and perfect, will of God.

Write the Scripture:
Word Study: "And be not conformed to this world"

Seek

1. What is God speaking to you regarding this Scripture?

2. What questions or revelation do you seek to know?

3. What is the principle to be learned?

4. Write out a short affirmation to help you remember the principle that you have learned.

Apply

1. How does this passage apply to my life? (past or present)

Share

1. How can I share the principle with others in a practical way?

Journal additional thoughts here:

_____

_____

_____

_____

_____

Day Six Journey: Dare To Be Different

"And be not conformed to this world"

As long as you conform to the standards of this world, you will never experience true Oneness with God. The power of walking in a renewed mind is greater than the pressure to conform. Feeling the need to conform stems from the desire to fit in. But we were not called to fit in. We are called to stand out. In 1 Peter 2:9, it states that "We are a chosen generation, a royal priesthood, an holy nation, a peculiar people, that ye should shew forth the praises of him who called you out of darkness into his marvelous light." Conformed people only shine the light on themselves. Transformed people show forth the light of Christ.

Dare to be different. Peculiar people belong to God, not the world. Your identity is found in the One who birthed you.

S.A.S. Principle

Romans 12:2 ~ And be not conformed to this world: but be ye transformed by the renewing of your mind, that ye may prove what is that good, and acceptable, and perfect, will of God.

Write the Scripture:
Word Study: "And be not conformed to this world"

Seek

1.   What is God speaking to you regarding this Scripture?

2.   What questions or revelation do you seek to know?

3.   What is the principle to be learned?

4.   Write out a short affirmation to help you remember the principle that you have learned.

Apply

1.   How does this passage apply to my life? (past or present)

Share

1.   How can I share the principle with others in a practical way?

Journal additional thoughts here:

_____

_____

_____

_____

_____

"And be not conformed to this world"

God has a frame fashioned specifically for you. The frame is called your identity and all that He created you to be fills it. What are some of the things God filled you with?

Ephesians 2:10 states you are God's masterpiece. For we are his workmanship, created in Christ Jesus for good works, which God already prepared that we should walk in them.

You can't walk in the ways of the world and the ways of God simultaneously. Oftentimes, our identity is wrapped up in what we do. We are the divine product of God. And God does not want us to conform or submit to become a by-product of the world. We were created for a divine purpose to fulfill a divine plan.

S.A.S. Principle

*Romans 12:2 ~ **And be not conformed to this world: but be ye transformed by the renewing of your mind, that ye may prove what is that good, and acceptable, and perfect, will of God.***

Write the Scripture:
Word Study: "And be not conformed to this world"

Seek

1.   What is God speaking to you regarding this Scripture?

2.   What questions or revelation do you seek to know?

3.   What is the principle to be learned?

4.   Write out a short affirmation to help you remember the
        principle that you have learned.

Apply

1.   How does this passage apply to my life? (past or present)

Share

1.   How can I share the principle with others in a practical way?

Journal additional thoughts here:

_____

_____

_____

_____

_____

This week's summary

As we close out this week's devotion on this section of Scripture, it is important for us to understand our identity as new creatures in Christ. We have a new nature, but there is something that we are charged to do, and that is to renew our mind daily!
(Romans 6:6)

Journal additional thoughts

_____

_____

_____

_____

_____

_____

_____

_____

_____

_____

_____

Day Eight Journey: Follow The But
"but be ye transformed"

Our greatest achievement is for godly transformation growing from babes to sons of God. This process can only take place when we follow the "but". Last week, we talked about the first part of the Scripture, "And be not conformed to this world". After the command comes a contrasting, objective statement.

But is defined as "used to introduce something contrasting with what has already been mentioned". How can I prepare myself to discover what is waiting to be revealed inside of me? Let us take the journey of transformation of our heart and mind.

Godly transformation is an inward working of the Holy Spirit that each believer must go through and without it, we will always think according to our old ways.

S.A.S. Principle

*Romans 12:2 ~ And be not conformed to this world: **but be ye transformed** by the renewing of your mind, that ye may prove what is that good, and acceptable, and perfect, will of God.*

Write the Scripture:
Word Study: "but be ye transformed"

Seek

1. What is God speaking to you regarding this Scripture?

2. What questions or revelation do you seek to know?

3. What is the principle to be learned?

4. Write out a short affirmation to help you remember the principle that you have learned.

Apply

1. How does this passage apply to my life? (past or present)

Share

1. How can I share the principle with others in a practical way?

Journal additional thoughts here:

_____

_____

_____

_____

_____

Day Nine Journey: The Unveiled Face

"but be ye transformed"

Transformation can only take place when we remove the veil from our hearts. The heart is the controlling factor from which we see, hear and speak. As we begin the process of transformation, we must understand the importance of the unveiling and what lies behind the veil. Veils conceal, hide or shroud things that are yet to be known. There is a treasure chest of the knowledge of God that we will discover during the transformation process. What veils do you need to remove from your eyes, your ears and your mouth? List these areas below.

S.A.S. Principle

*Romans 12:2 ~ And be not conformed to this world: **but be** ye **transformed** by the renewing of your mind, that ye may prove what is that good, and acceptable, and perfect, will of God.*

Write the Scripture:
Word Study: "but be ye transformed"

Seek

1.   What is God speaking to you regarding this Scripture?

2.   What questions or revelation do you seek to know?

3.   What is the principle to be learned?

4.   Write out a short affirmation to help you remember the principle that you have learned.

Apply

1.   How does this passage apply to my life? (past or present)

Share

1.   How can I share the principle with others in a practical way?

Journal additional thoughts here:

_____

_____

_____

_____

_____

Day Ten Journey: Behind The Veil
"but be ye transformed"

The moment we say yes to transformation, the veil is removed. Things that are hidden leave us with a curiosity to see what lies behind it. To have a renewed mind, we must understand that all of God's truths are stored behind the veil. We talked earlier about principles. Principles are a part of the transformation process. It is important to go behind the veil to get kingdom principles for kingdom living. There is a light behind the veil that beckons us to enter in. This light can be described as revelation. In Exodus 33:19, Moses asked God to please show me your glory. He wanted to see God in all of His splendor. All of who God is can be found in His glory, behind the veil. The characteristics, nature, and the embodiment of who we are to become is found in the glory. When we go behind the veil, the enlightenment that we need is waiting to light the path for our journey to sonship. Your character is made in the glory. Allow the glory to process you behind the veil. True transformation takes place as we go behind the veil and allow the glory of God to process us.

S.A.S. Principle

*Romans 12:2 ~ And be not conformed to this world: **but be ye transformed** by the renewing of your mind, that ye may prove what is that good, and acceptable, and perfect, will of God.*

_____

_____

_____

_____

_____

_____

_____

_____

_____

_____

_____

_____

_____

_____

_____

_____

Write the Scripture:
Word Study: "but be ye transformed"

Seek

1.   What is God speaking to you regarding this Scripture?

2.   What questions or revelation do you seek to know?

3.   What is the principle to be learned?

4.   Write out a short affirmation to help you remember the principle that you have learned.

Apply

1.   How does this passage apply to my life? (past or present)

Share

1.   How can I share the principle with others in a practical way?

Journal additional thoughts here:

_____

_____

_____

_____

_____

Day Eleven Journey:
The Freedom of Transformation

"but be ye transformed"

2 Corinthians 3:17-18

Behind the veil comes freedom. Freedom from the old mindset. Yesterday, we talked about the glory of the Lord being behind the veil. We must realize that it is the Lord Himself, in His fullness that is behind the veil. And we come to God through Christ Jesus. Wherever the Lord is, there is freedom. The light of the glory of God enlightens and renews the mind. When your mind is free, your life can be transformed because you can now see what direction you need to go in. When our hearts are set free from the bondage of sin, we can now run with God, fulfilling His laws and precepts. Freedom allows you to see clearly the truth of God's Word. Just as you look at your reflection in the mirror of God's Word, so our lives will reflect the freedom of transformation.

S.A.S. Principle

*Romans 12:2 ~ And be not conformed to this world: **but be ye transformed** by the renewing of your mind, that ye may prove what is that good, and acceptable, and perfect, will of God.*

Write the Scripture:

Word Study: "but be ye transformed"

Seek

1. What is God speaking to you regarding this Scripture?

2. What questions or revelation do you seek to know?

3. What is the principle to be learned?

4. Write out a short affirmation to help you remember the principle that you have learned.

Apply

1. How does this passage apply to my life? (past or present)

Share

1. How can I share the principle with others in a practical way?

Journal additional thoughts here:

_____

_____

_____

_____

_____

Day Twelve Journey: Transformed Eyes
"but be ye transformed"

Matthew 6:21-22

Before we entered the veil, we were in a state of spiritual blindness. But once we entered behind the veil, our eyes received a spiritual circumcision. We are now able to behold the fullness of who God in Matthew 6:21-22.

At our new birth, our eyes are made new by removing the filter for how we viewed life. Our eyes are important to our entire body. Our eyes are the first spiritual faculties to receive enlightenment. Why? As long as you can see, you will know which way to go. If your ears are opened first, you will still stumble because of the lack of sight. If your mouth is opened first, it doesn't have the power or the ability to guide you. Therefore, our eyes must first be enlightened because they point the way in which we are called to walk. We must have spiritual 20/20 vision. The first thing that happened when the veil is removed was our capacity to see and reflect the glory of god. What you see, you reflect.

S.A.S. Principle

Romans 12:2 ~ And be not conformed to this world: **but be ye transformed** *by the renewing of your mind, that ye may prove what is that good, and acceptable, and perfect, will of God.*

_____

_____

_____

_____

_____

_____

_____

_____

_____

_____

_____

_____

_____

_____

_____

_____

_____

Write the Scripture:

Word Study: "but be ye transformed"

Seek

1.   What is God speaking to you regarding this Scripture?

2.   What questions or revelation do you seek to know?

3.   What is the principle to be learned?

4.   Write out a short affirmation to help you remember the principle that you have learned.

Apply

1.   How does this passage apply to my life? (past or present)

Share

1.   How can I share the principle with others in a practical way?

Journal additional thoughts here:

_____

_____

_____

_____

_____

Day Thirteen Journey: Transformed Ears

"but be ye transformed"

Ezekiel 12:2

Before coming behind the veil, we lived a life of disobedience, in complete darkness and ignorance to life with God. We had ears but could not hear. Romans 10:17 states, "Faith comes by hearing and hearing by the Word of God." For faith to work, we must have the Word of God in our lives. Rebellion stops up our spiritual ears from hearing the Word of the Lord. The Word of God is being spoken, but we willfully plug our ears and rebel against the edict of the King. Transformed ears are those that have yielded to obedience to hear what God is saying. As your ears are enlightened, you are now called to hear the instructions and take heed.

S.A.S. Principle

*Romans 12:2 ~ And be not conformed to this world: **but be ye transformed** by the renewing of your mind, that ye may prove what is that good, and acceptable, and perfect, will of God.*

_____
_____
_____
_____
_____
_____
_____
_____
_____
_____
_____
_____
_____
_____
_____

Write the Scripture:
Word Study: "but be ye transformed"

Seek

1. What is God speaking to you regarding this Scripture?

2. What questions or revelation do you seek to know?

3. What is the principle to be learned?

4. Write out a short affirmation to help you remember the
    principle that you have learned.

Apply

1. How does this passage apply to my life? (past or present)

Share

1. How can I share the principle with others in a practical way?

Journal additional thoughts here:

_____

_____

_____

_____

_____

Luke 6:44-45

Out of the abundance of the heart, the mouth speaks.

In our darkened state, our speech is full of darkness. Complaining, murmuring, gossiping, back biting, foul language, etc. are all examples of darkened speech. What we speak is connected to our hearts. Transformation of our heart will cause transformation of our speech. Transformed speech is expressed in love and the truth of God's Word. Transformed speech is a fountain of life and blessings, not death and curses.

S.A.S. Principle

*Romans 12:2 ~ And be not conformed to this world: **but be ye transformed** by the renewing of your mind, that ye may prove what is that good, and acceptable, and perfect, will of God.*

_____

_____

_____

_____

_____

_____

_____

_____

_____

_____

_____

_____

_____

Write the Scripture:

Word Study: "but be ye transformed"

Seek

1. What is God speaking to you regarding this Scripture?

2. What questions or revelation do you seek to know?

3. What is the principle to be learned?

4. Write out a short affirmation to help you remember the principle that you have learned.

Apply

1. How does this passage apply to my life? (past or present)

Share

1. How can I share the principle with others in a practical way?

Journal additional thoughts here:

_____

_____

_____

_____

_____

This week's summary

As we close out this week's devotion on this section of Scripture, it is important for us to guard our eyes, ears and mouth (Proverbs 4:23-27).

Journal additional thoughts

_____

_____

_____

_____

_____

_____

_____

_____

_____

_____

_____

_____

"by the renewing of your mind"

Ezekiel 12:2

Every transformation needs the proper agent in order for it to be effective. The necessary agent is in the actual renewing of your mind. Renewal brings distinctive character changes, which are different from the unrenewed mind. As we go behind the veil, we enter a new life in Christ.

S.A.S. Principle

Romans 12:2 ~ And be not conformed to this world: but be ye transformed by the renewing of your mind, that ye may prove what is that good, and acceptable, and perfect, will of God.

_____

_____

_____

_____

_____

_____

_____

_____

_____

_____

_____

_____

_____

Write the Scripture:

Word Study: "by the renewing of your mind"

Seek

1. What is God speaking to you regarding this Scripture?

2. What questions or revelation do you seek to know?

3. What is the principle to be learned?

4. Write out a short affirmation to help you remember the principle that you have learned.

Apply

1. How does this passage apply to my life? (past or present)

Share

1. How can I share the principle with others in a practical way?

Journal additional thoughts here:

_____

_____

_____

_____

_____

Ephesians 4:22-24

What does it mean to be renewed in the spirit of our mind? Spirit here is the Greek word pneuma, meaning the breath of God, in motion. When God breathed into the nostrils of Adam, he gave him the breath of life, and he became a living soul (Genesis 2:7). There is movement in the spirit of the mind from the old way of thinking to the new way of thinking. And it is by this spirit that we renew our minds. We also notice that Adam received his marching orders prior to being made a living soul. So, it is in this Romans 12:2. We have been instructed to 1. Be not conformed to this world, and 2. But be ye transformed. Now we are given the process of how this is to take place. As we follow the Spirit of God, our thinking changes its direction and causes us to shift our mindset into the mind of Christ. There is a flow in the renewal that, when done in the Spirit of God, changes how we think.

S.A.S. Principle

Romans 12:2 ~ And be not conformed to this world: but be ye transformed by the renewing of your mind, that ye may prove what is that good, and acceptable, and perfect, will of God.

Write the Scripture:
Word Study: "by the renewing of your mind"

Seek

1. What is God speaking to you regarding this Scripture?

2. What questions or revelation do you seek to know?

3. What is the principle to be learned?

4. Write out a short affirmation to help you remember the principle that you have learned.

Apply

1. How does this passage apply to my life? (past or present)

Share

1. How can I share the principle with others in a practical way?

Journal additional thoughts here:

_____

_____

_____

_____

_____

Day Seventeen Journey:
Knowledge Produces Renewal

"by the renewing of your mind"

Colossians 3:10

When we enter behind the veil, we must take off our old self. But we must also put on the new self. How do we do this? Yesterday we talked about the spirit of the mind and it being a process. Today we will look at one step in the process. Genesis 1:26 states that we are made in the image of God. But if we have never encountered our Creator, we don't know who He is, what He is like or how He operates. Inside the spirit of the mind is the knowledge of who our Creator is. As we look at His image, there is a pattern that has been laid out for us to follow. The spirit of our mind doesn't just blow aimlessly. It blows within the pattern of the Creator. It is important for us to come to the knowledge of who God is if we are to be His expressed image in the earth. The more knowledge that we have of Him, the more renewal we will experience in the spirit of our mind. There is a full recognition of Christ that brings about mind renewal. The more we acknowledge Christ, and what He done for us will produce the knowledge needed to see our minds renewed.

S.A.S. Principle

Romans 12:2 ~ And be not conformed to this world: but be ye transformed by the renewing of your mind, that ye may prove what is that good, and acceptable, and perfect, will of God.

Write the Scripture:
Word Study: "by the renewing of your mind"

Seek

1.   What is God speaking to you regarding this Scripture?

2.   What questions or revelation do you seek to know?

3.   What is the principle to be learned?

4.   Write out a short affirmation to help you remember the principle that you have learned.

Apply

1.   How does this passage apply to my life? (past or present)

Share

1.   How can I share the principle with others in a practical way?

Journal additional thoughts here:

_____

_____

_____

_____

_____

Day Eighteen Journey:
Knowing Christ Above All Else

"by the renewing of your mind"

Philippians 3:8

The renewing of our mind can only take place when we are willing to lose every thought process from the old life. Our pursuit must be driven by knowing Christ above all else. When we understand that everything about Christ far exceeds our thought process, we will consider the old way of thinking like garbage. Who wants to live in a dump? You wouldn't bring old, stinky garbage into a brand new home and leave it there! But this is what we try to do when we don't renew our minds and leave Christ on the outside, or try to live this new life by using old thought processes. There is an excellency that comes with knowing Christ. A renewing mind produces the excellency of the Knowledge of Christ. It is the breath of God or Spirit that elevates the Knowledge of Christ above all else. Knowing who we are and what we possess causes us to soar like an eagle!

S.A.S. Principle

Romans 12:2 ~ And be not conformed to this world: but be ye transformed by the renewing of your mind, that ye may prove what is that good, and acceptable, and perfect, will of God.

Write the Scripture:

Word Study: "by the renewing of your mind"

Seek

1.   What is God speaking to you regarding this Scripture?

2.   What questions or revelat on do you seek to know?

3.   What is the principle to be learned?

4.   Write out a short affirmation to help you remember the principle that you have learned.

Apply

1.   How does this passage apply to my life? (past or present)

Share

1.   How can I share the principle with others in a practical way?

Journal additional thoughts here:

_____

_____

_____

_____

_____

Day Nineteen Journey:
Pressing Beyond The Beginning

"by the renewing of your mind"

Hosea 4:6

We can know Christ but never come into the knowledge of who He is. A lot of our beginning efforts of getting to "know" Christ are often masked in works, which do not produce relationship. We don't want to know Christ through our flesh, but our desire is to have true intimacy with Him. Ever reading a devotional can become the beginning state of knowledge for who Christ is, but he desires for us to know him intimately. We must press beyond this beginning stage of knowledge - of who He truly is. When we fail to pursue with excellency the Knowledge of Christ above all else, it affects our mindset and how we live our life. We will live our lives based off of surface knowledge instead of the depths of who Christ is, which can and will often lead to destructive patterns. Make the choice today to pursue beyond works and press into relationship intimately knowing Him and His ways. When we know His ways, our lives will mirror His.

S.A.S. Principle

Romans 12:2 ~ And be not conformed to this world: but be ye transformed by the renewing of your mind, that ye may prove what is that good, and acceptable, and perfect, will of God.

_____

_____

_____

_____

_____

_____

_____

_____

_____

_____

_____

_____

_____

Write the Scripture:

Word Study: "by the renewing of your mind"

Seek

1.   What is God speaking to you regarding this Scripture?

2.   What questions or revelation do you seek to know?

3.   What is the principle to be learned?

4.   Write out a short affirmation to help you remember the principle that you have learned.

Apply

1.   How does this passage apply to my life? (past or present)

Share

1.   How can I share the principle with others in a practical way?

Journal additional thoughts here:

_____

_____

_____

_____

_____

Day Twenty Journey:
Knowing God Loves Us

"by the renewing of your mind"

Psalms 103

Having knowledge that someone loves you changes your perception of how you view life. Knowing the love of God requires the spirit of understanding. We must understand that we can't only have head knowledge of what God's love is towards us. Earlier in the devotion we talked about the illumination that happens when our eyes are opened during the transformation process. This is the same enlightenment that is needed in understanding and knowing that God loves us. As we look at Psalms 103, we see the following: the description of God's love, the definition of God's love and the benefits of God's love. God's nature is LOVE! There is a difference between an attribute and the nature of a person. When we try to renew our minds without the understanding of the love of God, it will cause fear and a lack of trust when faced with the trials of life.

S.A.S. Principle

Romans 12:2 ~ And be not conformed to this world: but be ye transformed by the renewing of your mind, that ye may prove what is that good, and acceptable, and perfect, will of God.

Write the Scripture:

Word Study: "by the renewing of your mind"

Seek

1. What is God speaking to you regarding this Scripture?

2. What questions or revelation do you seek to know?

3. What is the principle to be learned?

4. Write out a short affirmation to help you remember the principle that you have learned.

Apply

1. How does this passage apply to my life? (past or present)

Share

1. How can I share the principle with others in a practical way?

Journal additional thoughts here:

_____

_____

_____

_____

_____

Day Twenty One Journey:
Knowing God Intimately

"by the renewing of your mind"

Matthew 22:37

There is a power from our thought process when the spirit of understanding is in operation. Knowing God intimately is crucial to our mind
renewal process. Yesterday, we talked about how knowing that God
loves us is one of the building blocks in renewing our mind process. In
Matthew 22:37, we see the greatest commandment left to us by Jesus.
When we love God with all of our heart, soul, and mind, this serves as
a three-fold cord which binds us to the Lord. Anything that is bound
cannot be broken unless there is a stronger power. But we just read that
the greatest of these is love. When we bind ourselves intimately with
God, we are one with Him. When we are one with Him, we also have the
Spirit of the Mind of Christ, which leads us to all truths (John 16:13).
We have our helper, the Holy Spirit, to help us as our guide, leading us
not only into intimacy with God, but into the truths of God's Word and
away from the old man.

S.A.S. Principle

Romans 12:2 ~ And be not conformed to this world: but be ye transformed by the renewing of your mind, that ye may prove what is that good, and acceptable, and perfect, will of God.

Write the Scripture:

Word Study: "by the renewing of your mind"

Seek

1.   What is God speaking to you regarding this Scripture?

2.   What questions or revelation do you seek to know?

3.   What is the principle to be learned?

4.   Write out a short affirmation to help you remember the principle that you have learned.

Apply

1.   How does this passage apply to my life? (past or present)

Share

1.   How can I share the principle with others in a practical way?

Journal additional thoughts here:

_____

_____

_____

_____

_____

This week's summary

As we close out this week's devotion on this section of Scripture, it is important for us to remember that God desires for us to know Him intimately. When you have knowledge of the object that you are supposed to mirror, it makes it easy to decide what is fruitful thinking versus that which is useless. A renewed mind always produces good fruit. (2 Peter 1:8)

Journal additional thoughts

_____

_____

_____

_____

_____

_____

_____

_____

_____

_____

_____

Day Twenty Two Journey: Proven Principles

"That ye may prove what is that good, and acceptable, and perfect will of God"

Over the past three weeks, we have learned several principles to assist us on our journey into the renewed mind. Principles are elements or rudiments, elementary knowledge of Christian truth or doctrine or a rule or conduct (Merriam Webster Dictionary/Bible Study Tools). When a truth is proven, it means there is a demonstration of said principle. When we begin to walk in the renewed mind, we demonstrate and provide evidence to God and others that our lives are indeed changing, and we are walking in the new man. We have a responsibility to demonstrate the glory of God. We are told that we are children of the light. And when we show evidence that we are no longer walking in darkness, we prove that we are God's children. When we walk in proven principles, we are able to be the glory carriers, living epistles read of men to those who are still in darkness. We are testimonies, and proven principles serve as an evangelism tool, especially to those that we came out from among.

S.A.S. Principle

*Romans 12:2 ~ And be not conformed to this world: but be ye transformed by the renewing of your mind, **that ye may prove what is that good, and acceptable, and perfect, will of God.***

_____

_____

_____

_____

_____

_____

_____

_____

_____

_____

_____

_____

_____

Write the Scripture:

Word Study: "That ye may prove what is that good, and acceptable, and perfect will of God"

Seek

1. What is God speaking to you regarding this Scripture?

2. What questions or revelation do you seek to know?

3. What is the principle to be learned?

4. Write out a short affirmation to help you remember the principle that you have learned.

Apply

1. How does this passage apply to my life? (past or present)

Share

1. How can I share the principle with others in a practical way?

Journal additional thoughts here:

_____

_____

_____

_____

_____

Day Twenty Three Journey: The Will of God

"That ye may prove what is that good, and acceptable, and perfect will of God"

Psalms 143:10

God has a desire for us to walk in the newness of life. This will include understanding the process of mind renewal. Only a renewed mind will understand the will of God because it comes from God. He desires us to walk in His will because it brings Him great pleasure. He delights in us when we follow the blueprint for our lives. But this can only be understood by the spirit of understanding. The will of God is a life of obedience. We are to respond to the will of God in obedience. For us to do God's will, we must first understand what His will is. We must be taught His will. There must be an acknowledgement of God. And we must follow in obedience. Here again, we see three principles that when followed, will prove the importance of the renewed mind. The will of God leads us into a land of uprightness. God's Word is the level ground that we need to live in His will.

S.A.S. Principle

*Romans 12:2 ~ And be not conformed to this world: but be ye transformed by the renewing of your mind, **that ye may prove what is that good, and acceptable, and perfect, will of God.***

Write the Scripture:

Word Study: "That ye may prove what is that good, and acceptable, and perfect will of God"

Seek

1.   What is God speaking to you regarding this Scripture?

2.   What questions or revelation do you seek to know?

3.   What is the principle to be learned?

4.   Write out a short affirmation to help you remember the principle that you have learned.

Apply

1.   How does this passage apply to my life? (past or present)

Share

1.   How can I share the principle with others in a practical way?

Journal additional thoughts here:

_____

_____

_____

_____

_____

Day Twenty Four Journey:
The Good Will of God

"That ye may prove what is that good, and acceptable, and perfect will of God"

2 Corinthians 10:5

God gives each of us freedom when it comes to choosing to follow His will. The fact that you are reading this book proves that you have a deep desire to do the will of God and understand that it all begins with the renewing of your mind. God only has one will. But in His will are good works. And we should always seek to do what is good. A renewed mind always looks to do what is good and not evil. Any time we have a thought to do anything other than good, we must do what the Word says in 2 Corinthians 10:5. If we lack the knowledge of God, how will we know what is good? We need these principles in order to do the good will of God. If you want to know the good, look at God's will. Only He can define it.

S.A.S. Principle

*Romans 12:2 ~ And be not conformed to this world: but be ye transformed by the renewing of your mind, **that ye may prove what is that good, and acceptable, and perfect, will of God.***

_____

_____

_____

_____

_____

_____

_____

_____

_____

_____

_____

_____

_____

_____

Write the Scripture:

Word Study: "That ye may prove what is that good, and acceptable, and perfect will of God"

Seek

1.   What is God speaking to you regarding this Scripture?

2.   What questions or revelation do you seek to know?

3.   What is the principle to be learned?

4.   Write out a short affirmation to help you remember the principle that you have learned.

Apply

1.   How does this passage apply to my life? (past or present)

Share

1.   How can I share the principle with others in a practical way?

Journal additional thoughts here:

_____

_____

_____

_____

_____

Day Twenty Five Journey:
The Acceptable Will of God

Day 25

"That ye may prove what is that good, and acceptable, and perfect will of God"

Ephesians 5:9-10

If the good is defined by God's will, it is safe to say that whatever is good is acceptable. When we are in agreement, we are in full agreement. When we do what is good, it is received by God with pleasure. Ephesians 5:9-10 states that there is fruit that comes from children of the light. We can test and prove what pleases the Lord by measuring it against the knowledge of Christ. God will always reject unacceptable sacrifices.

S.A.S. Principle

*Romans 12:2 ~ And be not conformed to this world: but be ye transformed by the renewing of your mind, **that ye may prove what is that good, and acceptable, and perfect, will of God.***

Write the Scripture:

Word Study: "That ye may prove what is that good, and acceptable, and perfect will of God"

Seek

1.   What is God speaking to you regarding this Scripture?

2.   What questions or revelation do you seek to know?

3.   What is the principle to be learned?

4.   Write out a short affirmation to help you remember the principle that you have learned.

Apply

1.   How does this passage apply to my life? (past or present)

Share

1.   How can I share the principle with others in a practical way?

Journal additional thoughts here:

_____

_____

_____

_____

_____

Day Twenty Six Journey: The Perfect Will of God

"That ye may prove what is that good, and acceptable, and perfect will of God"

There is a revealed will of God and a sovereign will of God. For this study, we will focus on the revealed will of God, which are things that God commands us to do. The revealed will of God has application to our lives. When we follow God's perfect will for our lives, we are complete. We also must know that just because there's a perfect will, there is no imperfect will of God.

S.A.S. Principle

*Romans 12:2 ~ And be not conformed to this world: but be ye transformed by the renewing of your mind, **that ye may prove what is that good, and acceptable, and perfect, will of God.***

_____

_____

_____

_____

_____

_____

_____

_____

_____

_____

_____

_____

_____

Write the Scripture:

Word Study: "That ye may prove what is that good, and acceptable, and perfect will of God"

Seek

1.   What is God speaking to you regarding this Scripture?

2.   What questions or revelation do you seek to know?

3.   What is the principle to be learned?

4.   Write out a short affirmation to help you remember the principle that you have learned.

Apply

1.   How does this passage apply to my life? (past or present)

Share

1.   How can I share the principle with others in a practical way?

Journal additional thoughts here:

_____

_____

_____

_____

_____

Day Twenty Seven Journey:
Recap Week One

1. Review your journal entries from Week One.

2. Have you noticed any shift in your mindset?

3. If not, what steps do you need to take in order to move from the old to the new?

4. Write your seven positive affirmation from each day below:

-
-
-
-
-
-
-

Day Twenty Eight Journey:
Recap Week Two

1. Review your journal entries from Week Two.

2. Have you noticed any shift in your mindset?

3. If not, what steps do you need to take in order to move from the old to the new?

4. Write your seven positive affirmation from each day below:

-
-
-
-
-
-
-

Day Twenty Nine Journey:
Recap Week Three

1. Review your journal entries from Week Three.

2. Have you noticed any shift in your mindset?

3. If not, what steps do you need to take in order to move from the old to the new?

4. Write your seven positive affirmation from each day below:

-
-
-
-
-
-
-

Day Thirty Journey:
Recap Week Four

1. Review your journal entries from Week Four.

2. Have you noticed any shift in your mindset?

3. If not, what steps do you need to take in order to move from the old to the new?

4. Write your seven positive affirmation from each day below:

-
-
-
-
-
-
-

As we come to the close of this life-changing, devotional study, take note of what you have learned about yourself. Identify any thoughts in your mind that still need to be shifted into a new way of thinking. Take the positive affirmations that you created from each day and solidify your new belief system and walk in the newness of life. Remember to use the S.A.S. Principle as a tool to renew your mind in other areas of your life and to share your faith with others. You accepted the challenge and now it's time to go, do, and be that person that God created you to be! And remember to think like the champion you are!

Love, Blessings, and Peace,
Lady Jewels

www.ingramcontent.com/pod-product-compliance
Lightning Source LLC
Chambersburg PA
CBHW080518090426
42734CB00015B/3104